Summary of

Where the Crawdads Sing

Delia Owens

A Guide To The Book By

Fireside Reads

Disclaimer: This is a summary meant to supplement and enhance, not replace, the original work. It is meant to serve as an introduction or refresher and you are encouraged to purchase the original work for a richer undertanding of the subject matter.

Copyright © 2020 by *Fireside Reads*. All Rights Reserved.

No part of this publication may be reproduced or retransmitted, electronic or mechanical, without the written permission of the publisher.

Terms of Use: Product names, logos, brands, and other trademarks featured or referred to within this publication are the property of their respective trademark holders and are not affiliated with this publication. The information in this book is meant for educational and entertainment purposes only, and the publisher and author make no representations or warranties with respect to the accuracy or completeness of these contents and disclaim all warranties such as warranties of fitness for a particular purpose. This is an unofficial summary and analytical review meant for educational purposes only and has not been authorized, approved, licensed, or endorsed by the original book's author or publisher and any of their licensees or affiliates.

Attention: Get Your Free Gift Now

Every <u>purchase</u> now comes with a FREE Bonus Gift

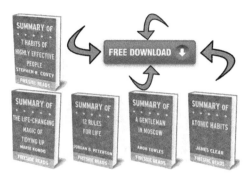

2020 Top 5 Fireside Books of the Year

(New-York Times Bestsellers, USA Today & more)

<u>Get it now here:</u>

<u>Scan QR Code to Download Free Gift</u>

Table of Contents

Foreword

Chapter One: Executive Summary of Where the Crawdads Sing

   Fireside Questions 1 - 12

Chapter Two: The Beginnings of Where the Crawdads Sing

   Fireside Questions 13 - 20

Chapter Three: Getting to Meet Delia Owens

   Fireside Questions 21 – 32

Chapter Four: What's Next for Where the Crawdads Sing

   Fireside Questions 33 – 40

Bonus For You

Foreword

Next to the roaring campfire is where the best stories are told.

That is our passion at Fireside Reads - to bring out the best stories and conversations between groups of good friends.

New readers can use this guide to learn key takeaways of the book along with forty thought-provoking questions that will challenge readers to think constructively in discussions.

By using this book, we hope readers will be able to ascertain crucial messages of the author for a deeper appreciation into the work that has been accomplished.

Take out a pen, Kindle or any electronic device to take notes and implement to make happen all that you will learn from the book. So start reading and don't forget to have fun – this too will acccelerate your *learning.*

Cordially,
The Fireside Read Team

Executive Summary of Where the Crawdads Sing

> *Did You Know?*
>
> The book, entitled Where the Crawdads Sing, was written by Delia Owens. Delia Owens has authored many books, and aside from being a writer, she is also a zoologist.

Tate returns to her life after having been away for a long time. Her brother Jodie returns to tell her about their mother's demise. Kya's life has been transformed by many events that happened in her life. She was able to write books about The novel, Where the Crawdads Sing, is a poignant and emotionally charged story of a girl named Kya, who inhabits the wild marshes of Northern Carolina. As Kya's life unfolds in every chapter, the readers are compelled to continue reading until they satisfy their curiosity.

    The setting of the story is the marshland in North Carolina. The area is in abundance of natural resources. The human settlement has flourished in the coastline area. Over time, different colonizers have settled in the area, exploring, and exploiting its natural resources. The first explorer who settled in the area was from France, by the name of Giovanni da Verrazzano. The purpose of exploration was to search for gold and silver. Since the purpose was not achieved, the French explorers abandoned the area. The Spanish colonizers explored the area and tried to infuse development but to no avail.

Lack of knowledge and research about the marshland topography impedes the effort to maximize the resources available. The marshland topography is harsh and not ideal for human settlement. Thus, it is scantily populated.

The author, Delia Owens, chose the coastal area for the setting for both practical and poetic reasons. The author is very familiar with the marshland having grown up in South Georgia, where she would canoe through waterways with her mother. As such, the place has a personal connection with the author, which inspired her to use it as the main setting of her novel.

The novel is divided into two parts, the first part is all about Kya's life in the marshland and how she copes with the harshness of life in the wilderness. Her childhood is totally different from that of an ordinary childhood experienced by the young girls in the surrounding communities along the marshland. The second part of the novel features the death of Chase Andrews. It centers around the mysterious death of a popular man in the area and the drama revolving around the blame and public scrutiny, which befalls Kya.

The story begins in 1952. Catherine Danielle Clark, known as "Kya" is left alone at the young age of six. Her mother has not returned home after leaving them. Eventually, all four of her siblings disappear from their home due to their father's physical abuse, leaving Kya alone with her drunkard father. Kya's father is a drunk and a gambler and is unfit to care for Kya.. As such, he too later abandons her. Leaving her entirely alone in their marshland home.

Due to her unfortunate circumstances, Kya is forced to look after herself from an early age. Having no money and no immediate family to care for her, Kya learns to grow her own food and to fish in order to survive. She eventually befriends two locals, Jumpin' and his wife, with whom she trades mussels and smoked fish for money and gas. Having been isolated from the rest of the population along the coast for her whole life, Kya is met with prejudice by those in society. She is labeled as "The Marsh Girl" atschool, and she is referred to as "nasty and filthy."

One day, Kya meets Tate Walker, her sister's former friend. Tate becomes her only way to learn about the world outside of the marshland. Tate helps Kya to read and write. They become romantically involved, but their relationship is short-lived as Tate leaves for College at the University of North Carolina at Chapel Hill. When Tate leaves, Kya feels as though she has been abandoned again. The reader discovers, later in the book, that her brief relationship with Tate plays a critical role in Kya's life story.

The second part of the book is about the death of Chase Andrews, the famous sports personality in the area, and a philanderer. In 1965, Kya was 19 years old when Chase Andrews found himself drawn to herexotic existence. Chase lures her into his world for sex but fails in his attempts. Not willing to give up, he then pursues her with the promise of marrying her, but he is still motivated only by his desires to sleep with Kya. Eventually they become romantically involved until one day, Kya learns that Chase had been lying to her and they go their separate ways.

Tate returns to her life after having been away for a long time. Her brother Jodie returns to tell her about their mother's demise. Kya's life has been transformed by many events that happened in her life. She was able to write books about seashells and seabirds and were able to publish them.

While she was away meeting her publisher, the mysterious death of Chase Walker has captured the attention of the communities on the coast. Kya was the main suspect. She was trapped by the local sheriff and jailed for two months without bail. The legal battle started, and all evidence to pin down Kya was overturned by her lawyer. The jury supported her innocence and ruled the case in her favor.

Tate and Kya got married and lived together until she died by the age of 64 years old. Not long after she died, Tate found the necklace Kya gave to Chase Walker and a poem. The ending suggests to the reader the possibility that indeed it was Kya who killed Chase. But Owen did not provide definite certainty that it was Kya who killed Chase Walker.

A major theme of the book is survival. Life is harsh and dangerous in marshland, the need to survive and to fight back in order to truly live. The story is also about independence and the beauty of being free to roam around in nature among the creatures and critters. Another concern is the maintenance of one's "freedom of spirit" in the face of adversity and judgement. Lastly, the novel deals with prejudice and acceptance. This is ever present in the racial and social stratifications of the book.

Fireside Question 1

The setting of the story is in a marshland in North Carolina. Kya's life is directly interconnected with life in the marsh. How significant is the marshland's topography in creating the theme of the story?

Fireside Question 2

Living alone in such a harsh environment from a very young age, Kya was able to survive independently. She learned to cope with her surroundings and to create a life for herself How does the title, Where the Crawdads Sing, relate to Kya's life in the marshland?

Fireside Question 3

The story teaches us about survival. To survive their father's abuse, Kya's siblings decide to leave to survive. However sometimes to survive, we need to stay and fight back. What message does the story deliver to the readers about the concept of survival?

Fireside Question 4

Kya's home is a dilapidated shack in the remote area of the marshland away from the town. In what ways does this impact the opinion of the town's people toward Kya?

Fireside Question 5

The setting of the story provides an ample reminder of social stratification. Those living in the town are affluent people, and those in the swamp and marshland area are the common criminals, the squatters, and the poor. How important is the setting of the story in developing the emotions and delivering the message it wants to convey?

Fireside Question 6

The people in the town ostracize Kya because of her living conditions. She is bullied in school, which forces her to drop out. How does this condition influence the personality of Kya?

Fireside Question 7

Kya befriends Jumpin' and Mabel, who have both experienced discrimination due to their colored skin. They become close and experience the same level of social ostracism due to their social standing. What makes this friendship important in defining their lives and how does their social status make the bond unique?

Fireside Question 8

Tate and Chase Walker are the two significant men who were drawn by Kya's eccentric existence. How do these two men define Kya's future?

_____
_____
_____
_____
_____
_____
_____
_____
_____
_____
_____
_____
_____

Fireside Question 9

Kya is tried and imprisoned for killing Chase Walker. The trial is controversial, and Kya is subjected to the biased opinion of the townspeople. In what ways does this trial heightened the social stratification in North Carolina's coastline?

Fireside Question 10

Kya was drawn to her natural surroundings. She found her independence and freedom among the living creatures in the marshland. What did she learn about fireflies that influence her choices in life?

Fireside Question 11

The jury decides in Kya's favor, and she is found innocent of the crime. After she dies, Tate finds a poem and necklace given by Kya to Chase. Does this circumstantial evidence suggest that Kya killed Chase Walker?

Fireside Question 12

Kya's life is extraordinary. At a very young age, she is abandoned by her family. She is subjected to public ridicule and biases, and she is implicated in the mur. Do you see Kya as a victim, why and why not?

The Beginnings of Where the Crawdads Sing

Did You Know?

Where the Crawdads Sing, had an impressive run in the world of fiction. It garnered the top spot on The New York Times Fiction Bestsellers in 2019 and The New York Times Fiction Bestsellers of 2020 for 30 consecutive weeks.

Delia Owen has co-authored various science-related books about her research and works on hyenas and lions in Africa. The book, "Where the Crawdads Sings", is her breakthrough work as a fiction writer. A lot of the book is based on the many years that she has spent in the Africanowilderness as well as a reflection of her passion for zoology. The book mirrors Owens' interaction with nature and how nature defines her perspectives in life.

The book is entitled, Where the Crawdads Sing, a title which conveys a lot of meaning. Delia Owens' mother once told her to go and explore the world "where the crawdads sing". This simply means to go off and wander. Explore the beauty of nature and dare to reach places where humans never dared to go before. Delia Owens has taken her mother's advice seriously and walked with purpose among the wilds of Africa.

Just like Delia Owens, Kya has been wandering through the wilds all her life. As such, she too developed a rare connection with the living creatures. She found her life among the fireflies, fishes, and seashells. The isolation that Delia Owens experienced in the wild is portrayed in Kya's life in the marshland, where she lived in the shack alone.

The similarities between Delia Owens and the character of Kya are not the only comparison one can draw between the author's own life and the details of her book.

For years, Delia and her husband, Mark Owens have been dedicated to their work in Africa. They bonded with the locals in animal preservations and continue to campaign for animal conservation. While working in Africa, they discovered some irregularities with the government practices that hampered the protection of species. They became involved with the fight against large scale poaching activities in Botswana and Zambia., Delia Owens' husband Mark, was then implicated in the murder of the poachers and was charged with the crime.

Kya's trial reflects the actual events which occured in the life of Delia Owens. The interconnection of the Mark Owens' murder charges in Zambia and that of Kya's trial in the book "Where the Crawdads Sing" is very evident except that the circumstances are different. The personal experiences of Delia Owens are very much alive in the book as it mirrors many aspects of her own journey of Delia Owens life with the wilderness.

The book "Where the Crawdads Sing" is a summation of Delia Owens' exciting, controversial and adventurous life among the wilds.

Fireside Question 13

The book reflects the experiences of Delia Owens while she was living in the wilds of Africa. She was isolated in Africa for a long time while doing her research. What are the significant turning points in Delia Owens' life that are reflected in her book "Where the Crawdads Sing"?

Fireside Question 14

The book is inspired by the life-changing experiences of Delia Owens. It also mirrors her mother's advice to discover the world out there. What's in Delia Owens's life that best represents the saying "Go way out yonder where the crawdads sing."?

Fireside Question 15

The book, "Where the Crawdads Sing" is the soul of a young and wandering Delia Owens. Is Kya a representation of young Delia? In what ways does she represent a young Delia?

Fireside Question 16

The book is the first fictional book of Delia Owens. She has written other non-fiction books about her experiences in Africa and about her personal accounts working with animals. How does her experience as a scientific book writer influence how she writes her fictional book?

_____
_____
_____
_____
_____
_____
_____
_____
_____
_____
_____
_____
_____

Fireside Question 17

Most of the story occurs in a marshland in North Carolina. Delia Owens devoted her time to working in Africa. How did the African experience of Delia Owens influence her choice of setting for her book?

Fireside Question 18

The book features the life of Kya as she lives on her own in the marshland. The vivid description of Kya's life is very well written. How did Delia Owens effectively create Kya's world and then accurately described it for the readers?

Fireside Question 19

Delia Owens is a zoologist. She spent her entire life working, observing, and studying animals. How effective is she as a fictional writer in portraying her personal interest in animals in her book?

Fireside Question 20

Throughout her life, Delia Owens has spent a considerable time away from civilization. Thus, she wanted to write a novel about being alone. Is the book, 'Where the Crawdads Sing" a story about how to be alone?

Attention: Get Your Free Gift Now

Every <u>purchase</u> now comes with a FREE Bonus Gift

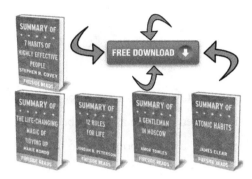

2020 Top 5 Fireside Books of the Year

(New-York Times Bestsellers, USA Today & more)

<u>Get it now here:</u>

<u>Scan QR Code to Download Free Gift</u>

Getting to Meet Delia Owens

> ***Did You Know?***
>
> Furthermore, the book was selected by Reese Witherspoon's Hello Sunshine Book Club in 2018. Inspired by the story, Reese Witherspoon is producing a film together with Fox 2000. The project is currently underway, and the screenplay is in the making.

The author of 'Where the Crawdads Sing" grew up in Georgia. Her love of nature was greatly influenced by her childhood memories in Georgia, where she explored the wonders of the woods while riding horses. Her mother played an important role in nurturing her adventurous spirit and her passion for discovering more about life. She allowed Delia Owens to wander in the wilderness. She is best remembered by Delia for the following words: "Go way out yonder where the crawdads sing." To honor her mother's memory, Delia Owens set forth her journey, as zoologist and scientist, into the heart of the African wilderness.

  The setting of her book, 'Where the Crawdads Sing", was inspired by her summer outings in areas in North Carolina. She wandered through the wilds. The lush marshland of the area has a special place in her heart. At the age of seventy, she can vividly remember her younger days spent in the said place.

Throughout her life, Delia Owens had a passion for writing and always envisioned herself to be a professional writer. But such love was set aside when she studied zoology in College. Delia Owen has a doctorate in Animal Behavior from the University of California, Davis. After her doctorate, she moved to African wilds with her husband, Mark Owens. In Africa, they worked as wildlife scientists in Botswana. They spent seven years in Botswana studying lions and hyenas. She lived with her husband in a very remote area with very little interaction with the outside world. They mostly met nomadic tribes. After years spent together in Botswana, they were able to write a non-fiction book entitled "Cry of Kalahari." The book was a bestseller at the time.

While living in Botswana, Delia and Mark discovered some irregularities in government practices. They criticized the authorities for putting up a long fence to curtail the spread of disease found in the cattle. This was because their actions endangered the wildebeest who were then unable to access the water sources. The couple expressed their grievances to the government but to no avail. As such, they decided to leave Botswana.

They transferred to Zambia from Botswana. In Zambia, they studied elephants. Mark Owens got deeply involved with elephants. While focusing their study on elephants, they discovered that elephants are the main target of poaching activities in the area.

In their effort to protect the elephants and other animals, they founded a social work program. They integrated the community in the preservation effort of the elephants and protection of the environment. They provided funds and introduced alternative livelihood programs for the local communities to discourage poaching of animals in the area.

However, the poachers in the area grew resentful of the couple's attempts to stop them. The poachers were aggressive and continued the illegal trade of elephants. Delia Owens' husband Mark was obsessed with stopping the poaching and got in trouble with the poachers. Mark Owens had made their base camp the command center of the anti-poaching activity in the area.

Then an incident happened where a suspected poacher was killed. Mark Owen was eventually caught up in the murder of poachers in Zambia. Mark was accused of murdering the poachers even though there was no truth to the allegations. They managed to get away from the controversy and after seven years in Africa, they return to United States to escape the possible repercussion of Mark Owen's alleged involvement in the murder.

While in Africa, Delia set up her own camp in the Luangwa River. She spent time studying the behavioral pattern of the elephants. Her passion for the wild never waned but flourished overtime. She spent every year hiking in the five major rivers in North Luangwa. She spent twenty years in Africa studying the engendered species.

Delia Owens has made use of her writing skills as she published her research and personal account of Africa. Her works have been published in the scientific journals Nature, Animal Behavior, Journal of Mammalogy, Natural History, and others. Her remarkable conservation work in Africa have been recognized and has earned a Golden Ark award from Prince

Bernhard of the Netherlands and the University of California Award for Excellence.

After twenty years in Africa, and now back in the United States, Delia Owens' passion for the wilderness has never ceased. She lives in Idaho and still rides horses to the desert. Elk, bears, moose, and deer pay her a visit in meadows near her house. Her life revolves around the animals whom she grew to love.

Delia's love for writing will never fade and so she intends to write more novels about the wilds. After the success of her first book, she is motivated to pursue her new career as a fiction writer.

Fireside Question 21

Delia Owens had a passion for writing at a young age. But she took up zoology when she entered College. What made Delia Owen abandon her passion for writing and instead pursue a degree in zoology?

Fireside Question 22

Delia Owens had a great time in the wild. For two decades, she spent most of the time isolated from the lowland. How significant is Delia Owens' experience in the wild in establishing the theme for her book?

Fireside Question 23

Delia Owens' mother allowed her to search for her own life, far and wide. That statement has been her motivation to go beyond the comfort of her home and take adventurous stints. What does the title 'Where the Crawdads Sing" mean to the life of both Delia Owens and Kya?

Fireside Question 24

Kya is a free-spirited woman who learns to appreciate the beauty of nature when she was isolated in the marshland. Is there a parallel between the life of Delia Owens and that of Kya or Catherine Danielle Clark? In what aspect?

Fireside Question 25

Twenty years in the African wilds is not an easy feat, but Delia Owens endured the long years of isolation. In the same way, Kya also lived in isolation in the marshland. What are the significant lessons we learn from the life of Delia Owens and Kya on how to survive in the wilderness being alone and isolated?

Fireside Question 26

Delia Owens spent significant time studying the behavior of hyenas in Botswana. Her research about the behavior of female hyenas is quite surprising. What knowledge did Delia Owens impart to us about women empowerment mirrored by the behavior of female hyenas?

Fireside Question 27

Delia Owens has a very real attachment to the animals in the wild. By learning and understanding their behavior, she learns to appreciate their lives. How did the connection of Delia Owens with animals lead to the movement for conservation and protection against poaching?

Fireside Question 28

As a scientist and zoologist, Delia Owens had a great time learning about animals. She observed animal behaviors that changed her world view. What behavioral patterns of the animals influenced the mind of Delia Owens about the world?

Fireside Question 29

Why did Delia Owens choose the North Carolina marshland as the setting of the story? How significant is North Carolina to the life of Delia Owens?

Fireside Question 30

Her mother is her inspiration in achieving more in life. It was she who motivated her to explore the world and traversed the less traveled road. What important role did Delia Owens' mother play in shaping her career as a zoologist?

Fireside Question 31

In so many ways, Delia Owens' life has been associated with Kya. Delia Owens has created the character of Kya out of her own life. Is there any significant difference between Kya and Delia? What are the significant differences between the two?

Fireside Question 32

Delia Owens once dreamed of becoming a professional writer. But she chose to be a zoologist and scientist. Her work took her to the wilds. Is being in isolation in the wilds a matter of choice rather than a destiny? If she chose not to be in the wild, would she have achieved her purpose as a zoologist?

What's Next for Where the Crawdads Sing?

> ***Did You Know?***
>
> Crawdads are freshwater Crayfish that look like lobster. Interestingly, crawdads "sings" by making sounds through their scaphognathite.

The book, 'Where the Crawdads Sing", was published by Putnam in 2018. The publisher printed only 28,000 copies of the book as they were not expecting that the book would be such a hit among the readers.

A year after it was published, more than four and a half million copies were sold. According to the data of NPD Bookscan, there was a decrease in the sales of adult fiction in 2019. In 2015, the sales reached 144 million, but in 2019 the sales were only pegged at 116million. The book, 'Where the Crawdads Sing", is an exception. It has landed No.1 on The Times bestseller list. It retained the top spot for 30 weeks while remaining on the bestseller's list for 67 weeks. The achievement of the book, 'Where the Crawdads Sing", is a big surprise. This only proves that people still love to read books despite the advent of streaming sites such as Netflix.

The book's popularity is attributed mainly to Reese Witherspoon. It was selected for Reese Witherspoon's Hello Sunshine Book Club in September 2018. The selection was a blessing to the book as it gave the book a most needed boost. The results were fantastic- as of March 2019, the book has sold more than 1.5 million copies.

It was also included in the Barnes & Noble's Best Books of 2018. The achievement for this book is remarkable as it also landed the spot as No. 1 for 2019 on Amazon.com's list of Most Sold Books in fiction.

According to Codex Group, the readers of the book cut across political boundaries. It captured an audience from different political backgrounds. Based on the study, 55% of readers are progressive. Meanwhile, 30% of those who read the book are conservative and 15% as centrists.

Reese Witherspoon has already given her word that she is producing a movie from the book. Witherspoon in partnership with Lauren Levy Neustadter and Fox 2000. Fox 2000 will own the rights. Delia Owen has confirmed that the screenplay is underway. Fox 2000's Elizabeth Gabler (and Erin Siminoff) will oversee the entire production of the film.

Fireside Question 33

It took a year and a half after it was published before the book established its footing in the fictional world. Where adult fiction has experienced a slump in sales, the 'Where the Crawdads Sing" sales have surged. What factors contributed to the surge in the sales of 'Where the Crawdads Sing"?

Fireside Question 34

Due to the surge of sales, many are asking about the meaning of 'Where the Crawdads Sing". While others find the title odd, others are intrigued by the story behind the title. Does the bizarre title of the book give an additional boost to the marketing of the book?

Fireside Question 35

Many claimed that Reese Witherspoon's endorsement of the book made the book famous. Its inclusion in Reese Witherspoon's Hello Sunshine Book Club boosted the sales to 1.5million. What aspects of the book made Witherspoon interested in endorsing it and turning it into a film?

Fireside Question 36

The book is appreciated by all kinds of readers. The impact of the book cut across political boundaries. Is survival, independence, discrimination, and triumph among adversities, appeal to the readers' popular emotions regardless of their political standpoint?

Fireside Question 37

Delia Owens gained recognition for her well-researched, non-fictional books. Her first fiction book has made some good noise, and four million copies have been sold. With this accolade, is Delia Owens a certified fiction writer?

Fireside Question 38

Some authors have to write several books before their books are chosen to be adapted to a film. Not all books are given such a chance. Since Delia Owens received enormous support for her first book, would you suggest that she continues writing fiction novels? And should she stick to her theme involving animals and nature?

Fireside Question 39

The book features some courtroom drama, suspense, and adventure. Given that she will write a new book, what genre will best suit Delia Owens' writing style? Would you recommend she write more about suspense with court drama?

Fireside Question 40

The sales of adult fiction books have considerably decreased in 2019. The stiff competition between published books, Netflix, and online entertainment has hurt the sales of published books. What adjustments should be taken by the author to win the widespread support for published books? Does the genre of the book matter to the new breed of readers?

Bonus for You

We hope you enjoyed listening to this guide from Fireside Reads as much as we enjoyed bringing it to you. Our philosophy is to always delight and over-deliver, so here's one final bonus for you.

Please do us a favor and leave a review. It is critical in helping others find out about this book. We would like to help them save time as it has helped you.

If you do, we will rush you these valuable bonuses: *(Worth $99 Retail)*

- **Top 10 Bestselling Fireside Books** (NY Times Bestseller, USA Today & more)

- **Top 10 Bestselling Fireside Audiobooks** (NY Times Bestseller, USA Today & more)

These hand-picked titles are the best of the market and can accelerate your growth and learning. Here's the next step to claim gift now:

1. Leave a review
2. Take a screenshot and submit to: http://o.cenasuper.com/o
3. Receive bonus as an instant delivery into inbox!

And that's it! You'll be back reading in no time.

Thanks again for reading and check out other high-quality summaries!

Cordially,
The Fireside Read Team

Attention: Get Your Free Gift Now

Every purchase now comes with a FREE Bonus Gift

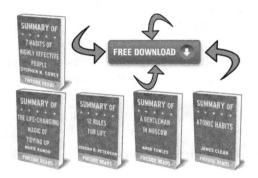

2020 Top 5 Fireside Books of the Year

(New-York Times Bestsellers, USA Today & more)

Get it now here:

Scan QR Code to Download Free Gift

CPSIA information can be obtained
at www.ICGtesting.com
Printed in the USA
BVHW040206210920
589261BV00016B/847